The Ultimate Guide to Dating for Women

Mary Davies

First published by Dog Ear Publishing
4010 W. 86th Street, Ste H
Indianapolis, IN 46268
www.dogearpublishing.net

ISBN: 978-1-4575-3262-7

Library of Congress Control Number: has been appliled for

This book is printed on acid-free paper.

Printed in the United States of America

It is said that to love...and be loved...
is the key to happily ever after.

I've often reflected back on my childhood days when I would pin a draping scarf atop my head, put on mom's high heels and walk down the hall, pretending to marry my teddy bear. Dressing up like a bride filled my little girl mind with the fantasies of my prince charming on his white horse pulling an enchanted carriage coming to sweep me off my feet. I dreamed of a big white beautiful wedding, the Cinderella dress, the colorful flowers filling the auditorium and finally my prince, placing the one karat rock on my finger. Have you ever dreamed of your prince charming whisking you away to live happily ever after? We look and go through life keeping this dream in the back of our minds, yet in reality, how likely is this to ever come to pass?

With all the media and pressure in the world it's difficult for us as women to keep our heads on straight and to protect our hearts from the confusion of men and dating. We cling to songs such as *Love is all you need*, *Love is the answer*, and *Some day my prince will come*, that only create desperate feelings that somehow being in love and having a man in our life will complete us or bring us eternal happiness.

What happens when *Some day my prince will come* turns to, *Love Rollercoaster*, *50 ways to leave your lover* or worse, *You've lost that lovin' feeling*? It's at that moment we're forced to step back from our fantasy and embrace the flood of emotions revolving around the loss of a relationship or marriage. How do we cope with these deep throbbing feelings of rejection or even abandonment? The confusion of a relationship that builds to this wonderful state of bliss then crashes seemingly without reason, used to overwhelm me. After years of relationships gone awry and a couple broken marriages I was led to make some life altering choices in the men I chose to date or marry. If only I'd had some knowledge beforehand I could have seen the signs and saved myself years of heartaches, rejection and abandonment. How many times must we come home from a date discouraged and whisper to ourselves *I thought he was the one* only to find out weeks, months, or years later that we misjudged.

Often times, and this was true in my own life, we tend to immediately rush into another relationship hoping to ease our pain and help us forget our most recent loss. Our friends and family lovingly offer dating advice and tell us "you were too good for him anyway" which just adds to our confusion. The tendency is to suck it up, continue about our life, and the next man that whispers sweet nothings in our ear becomes our new relationship. The cycle begins again and we fantasize that the new guy must be "the one." Our hearts become attached prematurely and we're in full bloom, until after we've slept with him and realize…he's not so great after all. Our failure to see the signs becomes yet another heartbreak, adding to the pile of broken relationship pieces in our hearts. How many of these can we handle as women before we either build a stone wall around our hearts and fortify it with an alligator infested moat or give up altogether and vow to live alone the rest of our lives?

Before I spent years researching the dating topic, I found dating all so confusing. In movies and romance novels, the guy always came back and declared his undying love for her...how could I have this dream for myself? Who does what when? When will he call? Should I call? How do I know if he's the ONE? How do I know if this is another empty promise or if he's telling the truth this time? When should I sleep with him? How can I ensure he'll respect me in the morning? I was so confused with all my internal questions, not to mention the conflicting information on the internet, in books, and from friends. What is a gal to do? How do we know who to pick? Which ones are good in the here and now but will turn into bad ones that emotionally abandon the relationship or find another woman later on? Are there any answers out there that we can grasp? Perhaps we need a set of guidelines to assist us to finding the love of our life?

I'm speaking from experience. I felt so desperate at times that I was willing to sacrifice my values and self worth just to acquire love. At the end of those types of relationships it cost me nearly everything. I repeated this cycle in my personal life for years because no one ever taught me the basics of dating. When we're young and in school, we learn algebra, science, reproduction, reading, and writing; all skills we will use as adults. How come no one has ever thought to teach us women about dating, relationships, or how to communicate with a man in a manner that would promote intimacy? It's not something that comes naturally. Our childhood fantasies are the only tools we have unless we're fortunate enough to have parents that taught us how to date so we can remove our fantasy blinders and choose wisely. I believe it's all about the men we choose and if we choose wisely from a healthy emotional view, we will have the love of our life and be treated as we deserve. The problem is, we aren't equipped to choose and we may not know how to choose.

As with many women, I wasn't fortunate to have a loving set of parents to explain the details of choosing an emotionally healthy man to date. I was left feeling powerless as I entered the adult world of dating and relationship and had no clue how to find a mature loving mate. Rather I had developed a warped sense of love from my father which lead me to search with seductive behavior to *catch* the wrong man. After more than one unsuccessful marriage I noticed a pattern with the men I was choosing to let into my life. I realized after my last divorce the pattern wasn't anything I could blame on another man, it was me. I had the wrong information! It wasn't the mans fault, yes the men did have responsibility in this, however I was the one letting them into my life when the signs and flags were as obvious as the nose on his face. The problem wasn't the men (yes men can be a problem) but the issue was my tainted views of dating, relationships, romance, and marriage.

Finding myself alone, yet again, I set out on a four year journey to correct my tainted views and transform my thinking patterns. Even though I had been a group facilitator and women's recovery life coach in topics like boundaries, forgiveness, and self development for years, I began searching for information specifically on dating and understanding men. I purchased numerous books on dating, went to conferences, listened to webinars, and interviewed over 100 men to become an expert on the topic and formulate a new way of approaching the dating scene. I decided I would NEVER marry the wrong man again and would rather be single and happy than married (or in a relationship) and lonely.

I began testing my new theories and noticed that the men I was dating were stepping up to the plate and doing the things I had longed for a man to do my whole life. I was finally being treated like a lady. I felt empowered and confident not just in myself, but in my ability to now choose a man who could love me the way I need to be loved. Men were talking commitment and marriage to me in a completely different manner. I had done the work and become a lady deserving of a prince charming. I discovered that my failed marriages had one commonality: **I was choosing men who exhibited immature behavior from the start. I chose to tolerate it and attempted to change them.** I was the problem. It was my distorted thinking that predetermined the relationship to be doomed. I was dating men that didn't know how to treat a woman, and I felt helpless to change it. I wanted to keep the man and change his behavior so I wouldn't have to face my loneliness again. It never dawned on me to walk away or communicate with my actions that I was not going to tolerate his negative behaviors. I was clueless! I felt as though when I walked away a man wouldn't chase me and prove his love to me. I needed some tools to better evaluate if he was a man of substance that would actually arise to the occasion and desire me, the woman of his dreams. I was so ignorant that I couldn't even imagine a man would want to fix things on his own. I needed help! I didn't know how to decide if a man was emotionally mature or should be tossed back out to sea with the other fish.

What if you had the tools before you dated a man, coupled with the ability to determine if he has what it takes to be in **your** life. What would happen if you were the one choosing him, not vice versa? I've discovered that when I'm feeling lonely and tired of dating is when I'm the most vulnerable to choosing an immature man that will never rise to the occasion of dating a quality lady. I needed to change **me** in order to change the outcome of my dating relationships. If I desired quality, I needed to become quality.

I began sharing my earthshaking information with the women in my groups and began offering advice and tips when they spoke of the emotionally distant man they were currently dating. Finally I launched my full dating program for women who were seeking to date or actively in a struggling relationship or marriage. The results were amazing and lives were being transformed. Men began flocking to the women I was teaching and some experienced more dates than they could handle. These women were talking of men falling in love with them and begging them for commitments. The women felt empowered to choose whom they wanted to date and whom to discard. I had offered them powerful tools and the results were astounding.

After such astounding results, I'm offering this book to women as a guide to the basics of dating. It's not meant to be a rule book or a one size fits all approach, however use it as a tool of how men and women think and feel differently about dating, relationships, and marriage. My hope is that I can assist by being a catalyst for you to find an emotionally healthy mate and experience true love that leads to a forever commitment.

.

SECTION 1

DATING 101

As women we want to feel; security in a relationship, a sense of belonging, completely loved, as a man's first priority, and feel a sense of stability in the relationship. Although it seems counterintuitive, a woman must offer a man freedom to be himself. It is then that a man will desire to provide the emotional security we need within the relationship. This balanced system goes awry when a woman tries to reel a man in or control his emotions, activities or him as a man. Oddly enough a man draws near and longs for a deeper connection when offering him freedom while simultaneously letting our insecurities be known to him. As women we must carry on with our lives, living fully and allowing the man to fall madly in love with the completely happy woman we are. This is a guide for women to totally understand how men and women operate differently in love and relationships.

**If we want a quality man in our lives;
we must first work on ourselves!**

The erosion of respect is nearly impossible to change once it's been established. Even though he checks out your bum and your face, it's all areas of your life that he's evaluating in his mind to discover whether you're the forever woman for him.

~~~

NOT EVERY MAN WILL LIKE YOU!

Just because you like him doesn't mean
he feels the same.
Don't ever try to convince a man to like you!
It's a subtle form of manipulation.
There are plenty of men out there; move on when a
date isn't showing you respect early on.
You don't need to try to like every man.
Just because he likes you doesn't mean you
have to like him.
Be honest with him and move on so each of you can
have the relationship of your dreams.

~~~

YOU DON'T NEED A MAN;
YOU DESIRE A MAN

If you have a great relationship with yourself,
your friends, and you are pursuing your
dreams, then you will be less likely to rush
into a relationship.

~~~

SLEEPING TOGETHER DOESN'T MEAN YOU'RE IN A RELATIONSHIP

You're not in a relationship until he ASKS you for one.

> Sleeping together and extreme intimacy prior to a committed relationship speaks volumes about you in his mind.

> What are your actions telling the men in your life? Predetermine a set of values regarding how far you go with a man and at what point you will allow which behaviors. Do this <u>before you ever start dating.</u>

If you haven't talked about it, ask yourself if you really want to do it.

Wait until a firm commitment is made before giving him such a precious gift!

It is your gift to choose when to give, whom you will give it to, and at what point in the relationship?

Feeling confident about your sexuality and dating prior to dating a man will help you keep your boundaries when the time arises for such decisions. Much heartache can be avoided by waiting until the time is right for YOU! The time is most always right for a man, and often even a good man won't say no to your candy dish, but it may come at the cost of the budding relationship. I've never heard any woman complain that she made him wait too long. A good man will wait with you.

With regard to sex; it only takes a split second to change the entire outcome of your relationship.

Don't become a "for now" girl to a forever man. Be a forever gal from the beginning to him and show him you're worth the wait!

~~~

~~~

CATCHING OR KEEPING A MAN ISN'T ABOUT DOING OR TRYING

Relax and just be the confident woman you are while allowing him to see and hear your feelings.
Be strong and confident on the inside (feeling secure in who you are and what you stand for).
Be soft and feminine on the outside (share your feelings and emotions).

~~~

WHEN YOU ARE AUTHENTIC WITH AND AROUND A MAN, HE FEELS COMFORATBLE AND CAN BE HIMSELF AROUND YOU

A man longs to relax and just be himself around a woman.   When a man feels that freedom while being completely accepted by you – his mind tells his heart it's safe to become attached and that's when he goes all glassy-eyed for you.

~~~

~~~

NEVER COMMIT TO A DATE WITHOUT LETTING HIM KNOW YOU NEED TO CHECK YOUR SCHEDULE

He won't mind waiting for an answer.

If you have a commitment with a fitness class, a good book, a girlfriend, or will be tired from work that particular day, etc., let him know.

Example:

> "I would love to go for a walk with you on Wednesday however I have Zumba class (or use *plans* if you have another date) and I feel so good when I go, that I don't want to miss it. I'm free on Thursday, what do you think?"

A man respects a woman that keeps true to her plans, wants, and dreams. Doing this never chases a good man away; rather it causes him to want you more.

He will suggest another day if he is in the mature man category.

~~~

TAKE A NO RULES AND NO GAMES
APPROACH TO DATING

Men truly hate women's *rules* or *games*;
they feel like manipulation to him.
A man simply wants you to be you!
Be the best you, you can be.

SECTION 2

MANOLOGY

~~~

MEN AND WOMEN ARE WIRED DIFFERENTLY

Speaking to a man as you speak to your girlfriends won't connect with his heart. When you use directives, tell him what to do, or attempt to control his activities, his mind is instantly triggered to hear old tapes of mom or first grade teacher scolding him. Once this shift happens in his head it's difficult for him to relate to you in a romantic or sexual manner. Rather, connect with him through brief feeling statements and he'll desire to keep you forever.

~~~

~~~

A MAN IS DESIGNED TO BE THE THINKER
IN THE RELATIONSHIP
WOMAN IS FEMININLY DESIGNED TO BE
THE FEELER

Start your sentences with I feel or a feeling word and
he'll respond with deep longing for you that leads his
heart toward the commitment you desire
(THE RING).

A man feels emotionally safe around a feeling woman;
and it's only then that he can fall deeply in love.

~~~

MYTH: MEN HATE EMOTION

Men love a woman in touch with her feelings, what they hate is a woman who blames him for her feelings or is out of control with her negative feelings such as yelling or calling him names.

Men love our feelings!

Verbalize them often. Preset some scripts you will use to communicate negative feelings to a man. Men fear the angry attack from a woman and having your feelings said in brief feeling statements of how his actions caused you to feel will prevent him from shutting down or worse, withdrawing from the relationship.

~~~

MEN HATE DRAMA

Drama is what we do when we're afraid of
sharing our true and honest emotions.
Emotion is what we are truly feeling and
perhaps afraid to share.
Verbalize your feelings to a man.

~~~

A MAN'S GREATEST FEAR IS REJECTION

He wants to touch you, learn about you,
and even smell you.
At the same time he's terrified inside that he'll say
something stupid and cause you to flee.
He's afraid of committing and losing his independence
yet he longs to be with you.
Men are fascinated with the complexity of a woman,
yet inside, he's terrified of her.

~~~

~~~

A man feels your love through verbal appreciation just as us women feel loved through affection and reassurance.

~~~

Connect with his heart not his mind.

~~~

Men thrive on challenge and need to feel respected.

~~~

A man loves that you love yourself, care for yourself, and nurture yourself.

~~~

A MAN CAN'T FALL IN LOVE UNTIL HE SENSES THAT WE ARE COMFORTABLE WITH WHO WE ARE PHYSICALLY, EMOTIONALLY, AND SPIRITUALLY

He is drawn to a woman who lives with purpose
in her life.
If you aren't confident about yourself, he won't be
confident about you either.
He may keep you as a friend, but will separate you
from ever becoming *the one*.

***If you don't know who you are,
he won't know who you are either***

SPEAK MAN LANGUAGE TO HIM

When we engage his naturally thinking and problem solving mind, a man is more apt to do the things we need done or listen to you intently. We can't communicate to a man the same way we chat with our girlfriends, he doesn't get it. Use phrases that allow him to problem solve in your life.

"I could really use your help with….."

He'll feel like a superhero and listen intently to what you have to say.

He'll be honest with you and even state when he'll be available to help.

He'll suggest that you and he talk when he's finished his task at hand.

This is a powerful secret; please don't use it for evil (I wouldn't want it to backfire).

~~~

HIS ATTRACTION TO YOU AND FALLING IN LOVE WITH YOU DOESN'T EQUATE WITH HIM PROVIDING UNCONDITIONAL LOVE OR A FOREVER COMMITMENT

Commitment and true love is developed over time.

As we feel emotionally safe with another, we begin to remove our masks and reveal deeper parts of ourselves to each other.

You will either surrender emotionally to each other or create resistance.

~~~

How you communicate with a man will determine the intensity of emotion he develops for you.

You can't antagonize and draw him close at the same time

~~~

~~~

HE WANTS TO WEAR THE BOY HAT
IN THE RELATIONSHIP
AND
HE WANTS YOU TO WEAR THE GIRL HAT

This means:

He gets to be the thinker as he was designed to be.

You get to be the feeler and bring the softness into the relationship.

When the hats get switched, he tends to become uninterested or deem you as a *friend*.

If we connect with a man as his buddy we have entered the friend only zone, a place we never want to be with a romantic interest.

Connecting with a man with logic only causes him
to seek you as a friend.

Logic alone will not cause him to develop deep and
lasting romantic love for you.
.
He'll tell his friends how great you are but he won't be
longing to hold you in his arms or dream of you
at night.

**He needs to be connected to your femininity
and feelings.**

~~~

EMOTIONAL SAFETY IS CRUICIAL TO A MAN

A man feels safest with his feelings when he's around a
woman who is emotionally grounded.
He needs to feel totally accepted (excluding his
negative behavior, never tolerate that), totally loved,
yet totally free to be himself. (not a project for you to
work on)

~~~

What draws him into your world and causes him to fall
deeply in love with you?

Men are magnetized by a woman that is relaxed,
vulnerable, and soft on the outside.

Be that woman!

~~~

MEN ARE PERPLEXED BY A WOMAN'S UNIQUE ABILITY TO FEEL

He longs to feel as well and when you create safety for him to do so, his heart will be drawn to yours and he will begin to see you as his forever relationship.
~THE RING~

~~~

Men crave to meet the *one* who makes him feel safe with his feelings.

~~~

A man needs to know that he makes you happy.

~~~

NEVER MAKE A MAN HAVE TO READ YOUR MIND

He hates statements such as:

"What do you think I'm thinking"

Just tell him honestly how you feel.

Remember: No games, no rules, just honesty is what draws him in and makes him long for more of you.

~~~

ONLINE WISDOM

If he didn't care enough to fill out his online profile
from the dating site,
He may be in it for only one thing, or still in a
previous relationship.

MOVE ON!

Question: What would cause a man to pay his hard
earned money for a profile and then not fill it out?

THE POWER TO ATTRACT ANY MAN
IS IN LEARNING AND UNDERSTANDING
HOW HIS MIND OPERATES
WITH REGARD TO RELATIONSHIPS
AND WOMEN

Men are hardwired different than us women.
Men think and approach with logic and solution.
Women feel and respond with tenderness
and femininity.
When we use our feminine feeling hearts to
communicate with his thinking mind,
a beautiful lasting relationship blossoms.

~~~

IMMATURE MAN GUIDE

A boy in a man body will exhibit the following:

Make excuses.

Degrade you for having feelings.

Put your feelings down or criticize women and/or their feelings.

Ignore you.

Tell you not to feel or how to feel.

Fail to respond appropriately when you share your feelings.

Withdraw from the relationship when things get tough or emotional.

Learn to recognize when he makes these types of statements and if they are a frequent event - move on!

These are HIS problems, not yours.

NEVER walk on eggshells for a man; you are worth more than that!

Keep being the feeling woman you were designed to be and RUN from any man who doesn't see your feelings as beauty.

~~~
## THE FOREVER MAN GUIDE

What does a *forever* man look like?

A mature man will:

Share his hearts with the woman in his life.
Listen and embrace your feelings.
Climb over whatever bar you put in place and will
respect your limits
(both personal and emotional).
Take responsibility for their personal issues.
Listen to your feelings and feel like a hero when you
share our emotional needs with him.
Wait for sex and intimacy until YOU are ready.

~~~

~~~

A MAN IN LOVE WILL EXHIBIT
THESE THREE P'S

Provide-Men innately feel proud to provide for their woman and family.
Protect-When we are soft and feminine a man feels a deep desire to protect us.
Profess-He can't wait to share his love for you to everyone, and talk to everyone about you.

He will generally begin showing the three P's early in the dating process if he sees you as a *forever lady*.

SECTION 3

FEMALE-OLOGY

GET A LIFE!

If you don't have a full life, figure out how you want
to spend your time then go do the things you enjoy.
He will be more apt to fall in love with a woman
who has her own interests. Your hobbies and activities
also make for great conversation and a good man
wants to hear about your activities. He feels very
safe and secure with a woman whose life doesn't
revolve around him.

~~~

LOVE YOUR BODY

If you want him to love your body,
you must love it first.
If you aren't happy with how you look,
take steps to change it!

~~~

YOUR ACTIONS AND CHOICES WILL ALWAYS FOLLOW YOUR INNER BELIEFS

Take time to write out a list and feel confident with your beliefs toward:
religion, politics, media, music, love, sex, etc.

The next step is choosing not to date a man whose core values don't line up with yours

.

If both of your political or religious beliefs don't align in the beginning, move on quickly! Spare yourself the irresolvable conflict that will be inevitable at some point down the line.

NEVER expect a man to change his core beliefs for you.

NEVER change your core beliefs for a man.

~~~

Define how you will conduct yourself in life.
Define who you are and what your purpose in life is;
your conduct will follow.

~~~

Keep your attitudes in check.

Define what your attitude toward the following are:
the world, religion/God/higher powers, men, yourself,
work, ethics, etc.

Your attitude will determine how close a man (and
others) can move toward a relationship with you.

~~~

Define your internal values.
Take a moment to define your personal integrity and
what it means to you.
Your internal value system will determine your actions
and the ability to enforce your boundaries.

~~~

YOUR PAST HURT, SHAME, ANGER, AND PAIN AFFECT YOUR RELATIONSHIPS

Get help dealing with past hurts that have caused shame, guilt, anger or pain **before** committing to a relationship.

As women, when we have unresolved past issues, our ability to choose a mature healthy man who will treat us as we deserve to be treated, is tainted!

Commit to working on your personal baggage and **become** the woman he's looking for.

Be honest about your baggage;
if your pattern is that immature men are all you're attracting, perhaps it's time to look inward.
Sometimes we need assistance discovering what leads us to settle for undesirable treatment from men.

~~~

BOUNDARIES

If you don't have good boundaries in your life,
he won't feel emotionally safe with you or connect
on a deep level.

When we have unresolved past issued,
we aren't able to set good boundaries.

If this is an area that could use improvement
in your life,
perhaps looking into classes or books
would be of assistance.

~~~

LIVE YOUR LIFE IN A MANNER THAT WILL ATTRACT THE MAN YOU DESIRE

If you're not taking care of your body, don't have your finances in order, don't have a job, and you're looking for the ultimate handsome, prince charming... it's going to be a long wait.

Prince charming is looking for a gal who has her life in order.

Prince charming is looking for his princess;

LIVE LIKE THE PRINCESS HE'S LOOKING FOR.

Get your life in order and be the best woman you can offer.

Live your dreams, enjoy your hobbies, love your life without expectation that a man will make it all better.

Make it all better then a man will make a great addition.

~~~

DANCE AND SING AS THOUGH
NO ONE IS WATCHING

His heart will engage when he sees you
having fun just being yourself.
Don't be afraid to do this in front of him.
You may even spot him staring adoringly at you.

~~~

DEMONSTRATE YOUR NON-SEXUAL VALUE
THROUGH YOUR ACTIONS AND SPEECH

He must perceive you as valuable as a woman
before you engage in sexual activity
or he may flee once he's partaken of your candy dish.

If he doesn't value you as a relational woman before
you have sex, then after sex he won't have anything to
connect to and may grow bored and walk away.

~~~

Staying involved with the wrong man
will take you farther than you want to go,
keep you longer than you want to stay,
and cost you more than you want to pay.

~~~

RELATIONSHIP WISDOM

Women thrive on relationship and need to feel loved.
Men thrive on challenge and need to be respected.

~~~

SECTION 4

DATING 201
THE DO'S & DON'TS

DO'S

BE HONEST WITH HIM ABOUT WHAT
YOU DO AND DON'T WANT

When you feel secure, happy in your personal life,
loved, and relationally involved with your girlfriends,
he'll trust that his heart and independence are both
safe and pursue a relationship with you.

~~~
## APPROACH A MAN

If you've been eyeing him in the grocery store,
at a party, etc.

Guys are attracted to a woman with confidence enough
to walk right up to him and introduce herself.

Let him lead after that…and have no worries,
you haven't denied him the ability to chase,
you've just offered him the green light to do so.

Offer the green light and make it a less
f a challenge to for him to say hi.
His challenge is in keeping you interested in him.

~~~

FEEL SECURE WITHIN YOURSELF
AND SHARE YOUR AUTHENTIC FEMININE
NATURE WITH AND AROUND HIM

When you are secure with yourself,
he feels as though no other woman could ever make
him feel so happy and draws close to you.

He longs to be accepted by you for who he is.

Your personal security allows him
to feel accepted by you.

~~~

SHOW HIM JUST ENOUGH TO LET HIM KNOW YOU'RE INTERESTED

Most men are afraid to ask you out.
Offer him the green-light to pursue you.
Move toward him physically to narrow the physical gap
between you so he doesn't feel so awkward coming
to talk with you. (remember it's a long walk
of shame for him if you turn him down)

You won't be chasing or appear needy
when you're the first to say: "hi."

He is so wrapped up in fear of saying
the wrong thing to you,
he'll welcome your "hello" and begin to talk with you.

Men struggle with rejection (big time) so if you're
interested, just relax and say hi to him.

~~~

OFFER HIM THE OPPORTUNITY TO STEP UP AND BE CHIVALROUS

Without any words or gestures, just stand at the door (when you're with a man). A mature man WILL open it for you. If he doesn't catch the clue after several dates, ask him about it in conversation because the action of opening doors taps in to his innate nature to provide and protect. If he's not inclined to do this he may have some internal thoughts preventing him and you need to be aware of this in advance rather than spend months or years wondering why he isn't chivalrous to you.

~~~

USE CAUTION
WHEN SELECTING A MAN

If you are longing for him to do something
he's not doing and you've shared your
feelings on the matter openly with him,
reevaluate if he's ready for a relationship with
you.
He's not a project and won't be changing for
you, so don't expect it.
He is who he is today!
He's not who you think he **could** be.

THREE DAYS

A respectful man asks at least three days in advance for
a date and does the planning for you.

It's very appropriate to offer suggestions
when he asks for them, just remember
it's not your job to do the planning.

Example:
Where would you like to go?
Your response: I love pizza, Chuck's burgers and the
salads at Barney's are fantastic... What do you think?

This lets him know what you like and
gives him a starting place.
Never leave him in the dark and expect him
to read your mind.

I advise to not be the one setting up the reservations,
and doing all the work.
Let him do it! He enjoys planning for a
great catch like you.
Let him make the reservations, do the Google map,
purchase tickets in advance, etc.

Early on or in brand new relationships avoid spur of the
moment dates - it sparks his subconscious to believe he
doesn't have to work hard to gain your affections.
A gal never wants to be associated with the word "easy"
Even after years of dating and into marriage, he'll still
enjoy planning the dates if you let him from the start!

~~~

GOOD MEN ARE OUT THERE

Make sure the one you select is good for YOU!

Never settle for a man who *will do*.
Get to know him before you make a commitment
and decide if you are both heading in the same
direction in life.

Example:
If his dream in life is to travel to third world countries
with a back pack and a tent and live off the land and
you're more of an indoor or city gal,
which one of you will forfeit your dream for the other?

In the most successful relationships both the man and
the woman have similar convictions in politics,
religion, child rearing, etc.
Core values are extremely important.

Share what you like and don't like. Share what you
want and don't want in your life.
Make these a part of your regular conversations.
This helps him know who you are at a deeper level
which is the beginning of a deep relationship.

~~~

FOREVER OR FOR NOW

Clarify for yourself in the beginning if he is a *forever* or a *for now* relationship.

The *forever* relationship begins with authenticity and appropriate physical boundaries regarding intimacy and ends with the man desiring to spend forever with you and ultimately offering you THE RING.

The *for now* relationship is based upon what feels good today **without** focusing on the long term or developing a relationship that will last a lifetime (THE RING).

You're worth the forever

~~~

DRAW HIS ATTENTION WITH THIS:

"I could really use your help with...."

This breaks the ice if you've never met.
Allows him to engage his natural ability to provide.
Makes him feel like a hero (no matter if you've just met
or been together for years.)
Keeps him perplexed on how to catch this bold
woman.

~~~

CREATE SECURITY

Create security by allowing him space to move
toward you.

Allow him to initiate the calls; it sucks to wait,
but let him call you!

Allow him space to ASK for dates with you.
It comes across as desperate when you call him for a
date or volunteer date suggestions without being asked
first. Instead, allow him to ask you what you would
like to do, then offer him a couple ideas and let him
know how much you enjoy each one of them.

Example: "I'm really in the mood for a salad
but I also love pizza."

This gives him a place to start.
Avoid having him attempt to read your mind.
If you don't want taco's TELL HIM!

Return his calls when you have the time. Don't rush to
the phone when it rings or play games about how long
to wait to return a call. If you're involved in a
conversation, out with friends, watching a tv show,
reading a book, etc, wait until you are at a place where
you can focus on him with your feminine hat on, then
call him back. There is no rule or set amount of time,
just make sure you're completely ready to focus on the

call or text and are in your best frame of mind. He won't mind waiting and if you are too busy, he'll surely phone or text again if he's really into you.

Keep your texts to one at a time exchanges! Don't text him every five minutes or instagram what you're having for lunch. Keep some information to exchange when you're on a real date. And honestly, few people really care about what you made for lunch or what coffee house you're at every moment. Quit texting and instagramming men with every thought you have. They just aren't into it.

Give him space to create a bit of longing in his heart for you. Men are thinkers and they enjoy keeping thoughts of you in their heads. They aren't sitting by the phone waiting for your call or text (they aren't women). They've got everything they need inside their head! Let him long for you. He'll call you when the thoughts of you get so intense he's driven to the phone.

If he's texting and emailing only,
HE'S NOT THAT INTO YOU!!! Move on!

~~~

TAP INTO HIS MANHOOD

Make him feel like a man by saying the sentence below:

"I feel safe (or protected) when I'm with you"

Watch what happens!
You'll be amazed how close he draws when you
make a statement like this.

~~~

BE STRONG ON THE INSIDE

A man is deeply attracted to a woman who emulates
confidence from within.
He loves hearing about the obstacles you've overcome
in your life that made you so confident.

~~~

AMAZE HIM WITH YOUR INDIOSYNCRASIES

They intrigue a man and he wants to know more.

He just loves your little quirks and how you snort when you laugh or pick the tomatoes off your salad and dump them on his plate at dinner.

~~~

OFFER HIM A SOFT PLACE TO RELAX

Show him by being your authentic self that he is better off being with you than without you.
He can't imagine being with anyone else when you're authentic.

He needs a soft place to just relax and be himself.

You can be that lady!

~~~

HE WANTS TO CONNECT THROUGH
YOUR EYES

When you catch him gazing into your eyes,
allow the opportunity and bask in the moment.

He's attempting to connect with your heart
and emotions.

~~~

90 DAYS

Focus on building a relationship for at least 90 days
before becoming intimate or seriously committed.

Don't worry; a good man will wait!

~~~

SHARE FEELINGS OPENLY

A man senses when you're communicating
from a place of fear and insecurity.
Rather than hide your true emotion,
try sharing your fear with him then watch him
instantly draw closer to you.

~~~

WHY DIDN'T HE CALL ME BACK?

We had such a great time on our date.

Perhaps he's overwhelmed by how secure you are and feels you are out of his league.

Perhaps he's at a loss with what to do with the emotions he's experiencing because he's not ready for a real relationship.

Perhaps he didn't feel the same connection you did.

Perhaps he's looking for a *for now* relationship and you expressed that you're looking for the *forever* kind. Do you really want him to call if that's all he's interested in? Aren't you glad he didn't call? You are worth waiting for and this man didn't deserve you anyway.

Perhaps he feels this isn't a relationship for him. No matter how amazing you, are if he's not ready for a committed relationship, nothing you do will suddenly turn him into the mature man you need.

Instead of wondering if you did something wrong or "why didn't he like me" try looking at this realistically. Not all men will like you. You may not like all men. Neither of those is the end of the world. No matter how dapper he looked, smelled or how great his manners and job are, move on early and remember the joy of the one or two dates you had; he's already moved on!

When we limit ourselves to one man it's just too much pressure to feel a plethora of feelings for him. Instead, keep your options open until one man makes you have butterfly in your stomach and you desire him as much as he desires you.

Think about this:
out of all the people in the world how many of them are your friends? Just a handful I presume. So out of all the men available in the world, what causes you to want a relationship with the **only one** you've had a date with in the past month?

Keep your options open and date others until HE asks you specifically for an exclusive relationship. If he hasn't asked, he isn't exclusive with you either.

Just because you went on a date or two YOU'RE NOT IN A RELATIONSHIP!!! Not to him and not in reality.

Intimacy and sex don't equate with a relationship either. Again, he must ask you specifically for a relationship before it becomes a reality for him. Never assume you and he are in a relationship just because you've kissed, had sex, connected, spent the night at his house, or exchanged *I love you's*.

If he didn't ask, you're not exclusive.

HE MUST ASK YOU TO BE EXCLUSIVE!

When he starts to get gooey feelings for you, be patient and trust that he'll ask.

~~~

GIVE HIM TIME TO THINK

Men spend a lot of time thinking and trying to rationalize themselves out of being in a relationship. When you are the feminine and authentic woman he craves and are patient while he's in his thinking mode, his heart will eventually win him over and he'll BEG you for a commitment.

Just because a man shows distant behavior, doesn't mean he's lost interest in you. Allowing him space to do his *man thinking* will cause him to eventually draw close and crave only you.

When a man feels understood by a woman, he can't stop thinking about her and longs to have her by his side forever.

DON'TS

~~~

DON'T HAVE SEX TOO SOON

Premature intimacy will never secure his feelings
or love for you.

I've never heard a woman say:

"I sure wish I'd slept with him sooner."

DON'T ASSUME HE'S INTO YOU

If he is texting you and not calling,
then he's not into you!
He likes you but he's not thinking
about a relationship with you.
Move on ladies! Move on!

~~~

Quit wondering if HE likes you and decide
if YOU like him.
Change your old thought pattern and you will feel free
to make a wise choice in men rather than settling for
the first guy that whispers "I love you" in your ear.

~~~

DON'T CAPTURE HIM WITH
MANIPULATING BEHAVIOR

Don't attempt to capture him with sex, beauty,
advice, doting on him, creating romance,
or overly pleasing him.
These things cause him to feel unmanly
and manipulated.

He wants to do the chasing!

If you are being your awesome, feminine feeling self,
he will do these things on his own because you've
touched him at his heart and feeling level not because
you've manipulated him into them.

Men can see a woman's dating strategy and games a
mile away.
It's not about having a strategy to win him;
it's about being the feminine and authentic woman you
were created to be.

Beauty and sex will likely draw him in
but will NEVER lead him into a genuinely loving and
authentic relationship.

~~~

DON'T MAKE HIM YOUR PRIORITY

Don't answer his texts and calls instantaneously. Don't play games or make him wait for a response. It's not about rules or time frames. Just remember to keep true to the moment (you're activities, the people your spending time with, or driving); and answer him when you have the opportunity to focus on what you really want to say.

Savor the text or email he sent, absorb it, and feel it...then respond in time.

If he's a keeper, he won't mind waiting for the response.
You're worth it!

~~~

The *for now* relationship will rarely develop into a
forever, so don't expect it!

~~~

DON'T PRESENT YOURSELF
AS A SEX OBJECT

Short skirts and low cut blouses may lure him,
but a man will have no idea of who you are as a woman
behind your sexy front.

He will gladly delve into your candy dish, but this man
will not see you as a forever woman.
Never allow him to view you as his sex object.
Be true to yourself and present who you are;
not what you have to offer sexually.

~~~

DON'T TOLERATE IMMATURE OR POOR BEHAVIOR FROM ANY MAN

Endless promises from a man are not part of a healthy dating relationship. Date others until he actually changes his behavior. You're not in a forever relationship until you say I DO.

~~~

DON'T COMPLAIN TO HIM

He despises when you complain about
your horrible life
but draws close when you share how you *feel* about a horrible circumstance.
Complaining is different than *feeling*.

~~~

DON'T SPEND EVERY WAKING HOUR TOGETHER

Refrain from spending lengthy amounts of time
together prematurely.
A budding relationship needs time between encounters
to breathe.
Longing for the next time he sees you is part of how he
develops deeper feelings for you.

A day or two between dates or phone calls is healthy.
Don't panic, he didn't forget about you in a day or two.
Spend some time with your girlfriends if you're
obsessing and need to get him out of your mind.

Couples that spend every second together or spend too
much time on the phone tend to have frequent spats
and fizzle faster than couples who give each other
space.

~~~

DON'T RUSH SEX

Don't allow his desire for sex to change your inner
convictions, get the relationship to progress too
quickly,
or sway your personal judgment.

Remember a man is naturally wired to want sex
right off.
It's not bad that he wants to take the relationship there
but a mature man won't mind waiting.
You are the one who directs the direction
of the sexual relationship.
If you don't want to go there,
THEN DON'T!

No amount of sexiness, giving, or convincing will make
a man look at you as a *forever lady*.

~~~

DON'T OVER SHARE VERBALLY
ON A FIRST DATE

Be completely honest about who you are
and what you want in life,
but there's no need to tell him your entire life story
too early on.

Example:

Say this:
"I would love to be married someday"

Not this:
"I'm so tired of dating and can't wait to have a house,
2 children and never have to work again."

Let him discover you over time like unwrapping a gift
(which is what you are.)
Leave a little mystery of who you are.
Don't offer false information or be so evasive
he can't read you,
simply offer the basics and give deeper information
as time passes.

Give a man something to wonder about!

~~~

DON'T PRETEND WHEN IT COMES TO VALUES

Present the right image of who you are and your
authentic set of values up front.
This will form the correct mindset of you in him.

Having your personal core values in alignment creates
the foundation of your relationship.

Your core values are important and if they don't match
his,
move on before your heart gets attached.

Don't settle for a man with opposing core values
the relationship could be doomed from the beginning.

~~~

DON'T WAIT FOR HIM TO CHANGE

Don't stay in a relationship filled with empty promises
that he will change.
Leave the relationship until he fulfills his promise.
Wait to commit to a man until you can have the
relationship you deserve.

This is your life and years wasted on the promise of
change are years you can never retrieve.

DON'T BE THE OTHER WOMAN

If the man you're seeing is married, separated,
or in another relationship you're allowing yourself
to be second.

No matter how well he treats you, how great the sex is,
or how much he professes his love for you,
he's emotionally unavailable. If you're looking for a
forever man, this man won't be him.

Here's why:

MARRIED: whether you like it or not,
you're number 2.
You deserve to be number one!
His first obligation should be to his family,
if it's not,
consider the reason you're attracted to a man who's
abandoning his family?
If you and he get married, what would prevent him
from repeating this pattern with you?
Ask yourself if you truly could trust a man who bailed
on his family whether openly or in secret?
Let him get a divorce first, if he's unhappy.

SEPARATED: How can a man be emotionally
available to meet your needs
while he's in the middle of a divorce?
This man is emotionally unavailable…He's emotionally
needy, but not emotionally available.
In addition, HE'S STILL MARRIED!
It's advised from many divorce books on the market
that one should wait from 1-5 years after a divorce
(this includes you)
before getting in a serious relationship.
This allows time to regroup and evaluate how to
choose differently for the next relationship.
When we bounce from relationship to relationship
without a recovery time between,
we tend to choose the same types of men repeatedly.
I speak from personal experience.

Let his divorce be final for at least a year (if not longer)
before considering a serious relationship or sleeping
with this needy man.

IN ANOTHER RELATIONSHIP:
Do you want to be his number two?
A man cannot have two number ones and believe me,
he's telling you both that you're number one.

A wolf that chases two rabbits loses them both!

~~~

DON'T BE THE MAN BY GIVING EXCESSIVELY

Don't buy him gifts, call him all the time,
or text him frequently.

Only give him as much as he gave you.
If he texted, text him back. If he called, then call him
back. If he emailed, then email him.

Giving more makes you appear desperate and is
considered chasing.

Men fall in love because of what you let them GIVE to
YOU not because you gave to them.

Men aren't women and don't develop feelings for you
through attention and gifts.

He doesn't need attention and gifts to realize what a
great catch you are;
WOMEN like the attention and doting not men.

He prefers a bit of space and to be allowed to come
toward you and give to you.

~~~

DON'T BE HIS THERAPIST, COUNSELOR, OR MOM

He will only see you as a buddy and will never envision you as his lover or mate.

WHAT IF YOU DO A DON'T?

It's NEVER too late to turn the page
and start again more wisely.

When in doubt, don't commit!

If you discover that you may be in danger, seek help
before taking drastic steps to end a relationship.

Use your verbal NO muscle
and consciously decide that you don't need to do things
simply to get him to like you.
Be likeable and the right man will like you too!

**Move ahead more wisely than before,
we all start somewhere.**

SECTION 5

WE'RE DATING.
NOW WHAT?

The keys to keeping him,
now that you're in a relationship.

Women need relationship and security in a relationship…evaluate if the man you're dating is providing this for you.

~~~

KEEP HIS MAGNETIC ATTRACTION ALIVE BY USING FEELING WORDS

"I feel….." when you communicate with him.

These words bring out your softness which is what a man longs for in a woman.
This is how you connect his heart to the relationship.
Without a heart connection a man will rarely stay in deep committed love.

When you use the *I feel* statement be sure to follow it with a true feeling word such as:
excited, happy, confused, sad, etc.
Try to avoid the tendency to say " I feel you….."
It may sound funny reading it here,
but I've caught myself in this trap before and it doesn't qualify as an *I feel* statement.

~~~

Make him feel safe around you by sharing your feelings instead of your advice.

He'll love the way you expressed your feelings around him and this will keep him thinking about you long after the date is over.

He'll tell you he's never met a gal that is so expressive and how much he admires that in you.

He will long for more of you.

~~~

STAY IN YOUR PINK HAT GIRLY MODE

He craves to know what you're feeling but when you spend too much time in the blue hat thinking mode he tends to switch and relate as your friend or comrade.

If he asks what you're thinking, try to answer with how you're feeling.
He'll be drawn into your female magnetism when you bring the conversations back to feelings.

~~~

Your authentic feelings expressed from your heart, make him feel safe to be himself around you.
Men have insecurities too and your authenticity creates an environment for him to let his guard down.

~~~

BE HIS LOVER

While it's important to be his best friend,
remember to be his lover not his comrade.

A healthy mature man has other men in his life to
guide him and have camaraderie
A man with healthy friends is a good man to keep.

Beware of a man with few or no close friends.

A man desires to share feelings and intimacy
with a woman.
Be the woman he can do that with and
he'll draw closer to you.
He'll want to spend all his time with you and less time
with his friends.

~~~

YOUR NEGATIVE FEELINGS WON'T CHASE A GOOD MAN AWAY

It's about sharing your true feelings with your man.

The feeling you're afraid of sharing with him because
it may chase him away,
is the very thing he needs to hear from you.

Tell him in a feeling statement
and at the appropriate time which creates emotional
safety for him.
Then he can let his guard down and continue
developing deep loving feelings for you.

~~~

STATE YOUR BOUNDARIES

Your boundaries stated in a loving manner will draw
him even closer, not push him away.

The word NO said in a pleasant and respectful manner
will never chase a good man away.

~~~

YOUR MAN WANTS TO FEEL *GOOD ENOUGH*

Extensive complaining of all the things he's doing
wrong will surely chase a good man away.

Practice your feeling statements regarding his negative
behavior with a girlfriend before you approach him.
Rehearsing first prevents our female tendency to
over talk, blame, or criticize.

Healthy feeling statements will facilitate change and
growth
in him when stated without the anger and blame.

Be his source of joy, love, and passion
and he'll need you to be in his life forever.

~~~

When a man knows that he's making you happy
in the relationship,
he'll feel incredible around you and crave
more time with you.

Your man will move mountains just to spend time with
you.

~~~

LET HIM BE HIMSELF

A man that feels comfortable being himself around you
will long for more time with you.
He'll never think twice about giving up all other
women, forever, if he feels comfortable around you.

~~~

If you desire healthy unconditional love from him,
you must have healthy love for yourself
and who you truly are.

~~~

When a man enjoys the role he plays in the
relationship and feels needed,
he will be more inclined to be attracted to you
physically and emotionally.
He will be calling you back!

~~~

CONTROL YOUR ANGER

When he senses that you can handle your feelings,
he feels safe to let his out.

This means that you present your feelings
in a rational manner,
especially the negative ones.
Men hate our angry outbursts especially
when they're directed at him personally.

Be sure to check your feelings and
use true feeling statements
to communicate overwhelming feelings with him.

A man doesn't typically respond to feelings
the way we women do,
and it sort of freaks him out when we go
on our rampages.

Once you've created this safe emotional environment
for him,
A mature man will be the one begging *you* for a talk
about where the relationship is going.
This man will truly want you and only you in his arms
forever.

~~~

CHALLENGE HIM TO CHASE

When a man feels like he's got the *maybe* or *perhaps*
from you, he'll surely chase you.

A direct yes given too easily could mean
you're an easy catch or desperate
(he gets lazy or turned off.)

A *no* could mean that you're playing hard to get or
playing games
(men hate that.)

Just be yourself and offer a playful maybe,
he loves a little challenge and mystery in his woman.

~~~

Be playful and banter with him regularly.

~~~

MEN ARE NATURAL PROBLEM SOLVERS

Tap into his natural desire by adding the phrase
"What do you think?"
after you share an idea with him.
He will feel like a hero that gets to play a role in
solving your problems.
He will also listen more intently when he knows he's
going to be included in the solution.

~~~

SOFTEN AN INTEROGATION
WITH THESE WORDS

When you need more information from a man about
where he's been or the like, which feels like an
interrogation to him, preface your sentence with

"I'm just curious……"

It'll soften your inquisition and he'll be less defensive
and more responsive to you and ultimately
you'll get the answers you desire with minimal conflict.

~~~

BE WILLING TO WALK AWAY FROM THE DISAGREEMENT

Show him that you're willing to walk away
when you're not treated as you desire to be treated.

Leave a room, calmly.

Say good-bye immediately on the phone,
then hang up, softly.

Let him know you're feeling confused by the situation
and need time to process your feelings, then zip it and
leave the room.

~~~

CATCHING HIM IS ONLY THE FIRST STEP

If you want to keep him forever,
then you must do the following:

1. Use feeling statements when communicating.
2. Present your authentic self with all your likes and dislikes.
3. Have true inner beauty to match your outer beauty.
4. Set and keep healthy physical boundaries with intimacy.
5. Keep your emotions and feelings real and present them to him without anger or blame.
6. Have healthy emotional boundaries and verbalize when you feel hurt by his actions.

Use these guidelines as a catalyst in creating a deep and lasting relationship with your man.
He won't be able to stop thinking about a forever commitment with you....THE RING!

~~~

HAVE CORE BELIEF DISCUSSIONS

Religious and political views are essential
to have in common.
Never change your beliefs for a man.
Only change them because you have adopted a new
way of thinking that really makes sense,
but don't do it just because it's the man's
religion or *political party*.

~~~

ADDRESS HIM WITH WARMTH NOT ANGER

When a man's hurt you, give him the opportunity to feel your warmth instead of cold anger.

Tell him how his actions caused you to feel rather than attack and criticize him for messing up.

Then hear him out and come to a conclusion as to what you will do if his negative behavior continues.

Patterns of negative behavior are detrimental to a healthy relationship.
Look for progress before committing to a man who exhibits hurt towards you.

It's not forever until you say I DO.

~~~

When you confront something he's done wrong,
engage him with your feelings,
then pause…(zip-it)
and allow him space to respond.

Try this statement:
"I'm confused about ….. could you help me understand….."

~~~

CONTINUE TO BRING OUT
THE BEST OF HIM

It takes the right kind of woman to bring out
the best features of a man;
be that woman.

~~~

It's your job as a woman to create an emotionally
safe environment for your man.
Give him emotional safety to influence him to stay.

~~~

Tell your man that you respect his feelings and let him
know how you feel because he respects yours.
This statement tells him that you know
he's listening to you.
A man loves to know when he's doing something right.

~~~

HE LOVES WHEN YOU TAKE CARE OF YOURSELF

It's not that you need to prance around in black lacy
negligees or wear tons of make up.
He loves you plain, too.
Just take great care of your body, mind, and soul.
He'll follow suit and take care of you too!

A man is in awe that a woman can take so long to get
ready or pick out an outfit, keep the mystery alive.

~~~

HE WANTS YOU TO TALK TO HIM
WITH FEELING STATEMENTS WHEN
HE'S HURT YOU

Share how you felt as a result of his action versus
attacking him.

This creates a heartfelt connection with him and the
mature man grows deeper in love with you,
listens to your heart, and acknowledges the pain he
may have caused.

He'll even be inclined to change his part
and ultimately,
draw closer to you.

~~~

You cannot appear authentic or genuine if you're
pretending not to be upset with him.

If you feel like screaming inside, he can tell.

Share your feelings before the date, don't ruin the
entire evening with him.
It's far better to have a difficult conversation at home
before you go out
or skip the date altogether and talk it through.
Perhaps cancel or reschedule the date until you and he
resolve it.

In the long run, a good man's love will grow deeper
when you are honest with him.

~~~

Holding your tongue on negative feelings rather than
sharing what's on your heart can cause him to withdraw
from you emotionally.

~~~

When sharing your negative feelings with a man, be
certain you've removed the attack, complaining, and
lengthy explanations prior to talking with him.
Lengthy explanations make him feel lectured
(like his mom used to do).

He will be more responsive and desire to
resolve the issue with
you when you're sharing only your feelings.

~~~

YOUR MAN WANTS TO BE YOUR HERO

When he saves the day or solves your problem,
let him know by saying:

"You're my hero."

He'll want to keep doing these types of things as long
as he's getting a positive response from you.

~~~

COMMUNICATE YOUR SPECIFIC
RELATIONSHIP NEEDS TO YOUR MAN

Here are a couple of great scripted examples that you can memorize and make your own.
These will not chase him away but will help him understand where you're coming from and what your expectations are for the relationship:

"I need to be in a relationship where I feel…….."

"I need the man in my life to……"

~~~

SOLVE THE LULL IN THE CONVERSATION

When there's an awkward lull in the conversation
with a man,
try using a feeling statement to get things going again.

Example: "I'm so excited to see the movie/
play tonight."

Then zip it and watch him engage with you
emotionally.
He will act upon your feeling statement and the
awkwardness will dissipate.

When we express a feeling in front of him,
it allows him to draw closer and desire to do
something.
he may look toward you, hold you closer, speak,
or stroke your arm.
When you've acted like the female part of the
relationship the lull can vanish!
He loves your feelings and your femininity.

~~~

LET YOUR MAN KNOW THAT YOU ENJOY HIS COMPANY

Try not to have an agenda.
He's not a means to an end, such as marriage.
He is a human with feelings and insecurities
just like you.
Authenticity is the key.
Say what you mean and what you want/
don't want and accept the outcome.

Enjoy who he is, as he is.

~~~

A ROUGH SPOT DOESN'T MEAN A BREAK-UP

A rough spot in the relationship isn't
the cause of a break up.

How the rough spot is handled could be!

How we handle conflict is what builds a rock-solid
foundation that is nearly unbreakable.
Rough times can actually bring you closer and
build on the connection
and bond of trust you're developing with each other.
Conflict is your friend when handled
with care and concern
for the good of the relationship.

~~~

A SECRET WEAPON

When you feel as though he doesn't listen to ,
try speaking his language when communicating rather
than criticizing.

Men respond differently than women
and have the ability to tune us out when we trigger
certain emotions in them.

Some men are immature and unresponsive even when
we speak their language.
If they're not listening to you the way you need or
deserve, after approaching with feeling statements,
run!

A mature man will listen to what you say and,
most importantly,
he will act upon it....when you learn to speak
his language.

Use short "I feel" statements followed by a pause
for him to answer.

The phrase "I need your help with something"
works like a charm too,
even if what you need help with is the relationship.
This taps into his "gotta fix-it" mode and he's all ears!

Understanding the man's language and response
system is like gold.
This is your secret weapon.
Don't use it too often or it could backfire!

~~~
# GETTING HIS ATTENTION

If he appears to care more about the ball game or his
computer than you on a regular basis,
it's time to let him know you need his help
with something.

Set a time that is convenient for both of you
when it's relaxed.

Use feeling statements such as:

"I miss the way we used to .........what do you think?"

"I'm feeling more distant than usual,
what do you think we can do about that?"

"I made a special dinner and am feeling insecure
about whether or not you liked it,
can you help me with that?"

~~~

DO THESE JEANS MAKE MY BUTT LOOK FAT?

Phrase your questions wisely.
Never ask questions that require him to perform in order to get it right.

Such as:

"Do these pants make my butt look big?"
"Why didn't you notice my new hairdo?"…and the like.

These questions make him feel worse than fingers on a chalkboard and ultimately freak him out.

Instead try:
"I'm feeling weird about my weight today can you remind me how sexy I am to you?"

"I am so happy with my new hairdo, what do you think?"

These feeling statement examples allow him freedom to get the answer right
and you get the results you were needing in the first place.
Everybody wins!

I realize this is all semantics; however, men speak, hear, and respond differently than women.
Evaluate the difference in him when you try wording something different.

If you need to use these as a script, please do, they are tried and true and have worked great for me and countless others.

The point is: MEN HATE TO FEEL
PUT ON THE SPOT.

They simply need to know the answer will ultimately make you happy.

All your man knows in the jeans situation is that you look sexy to him or he wouldn't be there with you. If you truly don't know if your butt looks big in those jeans, get a mirror and check it out for yourself or ask your girlfriend. It's not bad for him to respond in a way that keeps you happy. He's not lying.

It's just the MAN way of thinking.

Men just wants you to feel happy.

If you want a man in your life, the good ones come with *man thinking*. Attempting to get him to think and respond like a woman is going to backfire in the long run and he uld become passive with his answers over time.

~~~

MEASURE OF A MAN

It's said that the measure of a man is found in the
countenance of his woman.
If you're not glowing when you're around him…
something may not be kosher in the relationship.

A woman in love is all lit up inside and out.

~~~

CHOOSE YOUR WORDS CAREFULLY

You cannot antagonize and draw him close…
simultaneously.

Ask yourself if your words are causing him to become
defensive or passive,
then change them if necessary!

~~~

SOMETHING COULD BE AMISS

When you feel abnormally nit picky or naggy it could
be a sign that something is amiss.
When we feel emotionally disconnected from the
relationship our insecurities can drive our behavior.
Check your heart and see if some aspect of the
relationship's security has been compromised.
There may be a connectedness issue in the background
of your behavior.

~~~

HE ACTS HOT AND COLD
ON A REGULAR BASIS

A hot and cold man is an immature man emotionally
and won't treat you as you deserve.
Wait until the fruit is ripe before you pick him,
there are mature men that will treat you
as you deserve.

You don't need to be any man's fixer.

~~~

COMFORTABLE IN A RELATIONSHIP ISN'T A TICKET TO COMPLAIN

He won't be apt to stay deeply in love with you if you advise him, gossip about your friends, over analyze everything he does, or continually need updates about where the relationship is going.
He will listen out of courtesy,
but his green relationship light will change to an yellow caution light.

Remember to use the "I feel" statements to keep him drawn to you.

~~~

DON'T MAKE HIM WRONG ALL THE TIME

Try not to make a man feel *wrong* or he may withdraw
or hide his heart from you in the future.

Instead share how his actions caused you to feel
and allow him to step up and make it right.

~~~

KEEP YOUR OWN LIFE

Have your own life and activities and
draw him into those.

Develop activities that you enjoy together,
but keep some activities that just you and the girls do.

Refrain from immersing yourself into every aspect of
his life and his activities.
Rather, be his support as he goes out and enjoys them
without you.
When he returns from his hobby time,
he'll love knowing you're on his team
and that you've given him time to enjoy his freedom.

Men hate feeling as though they've lost or
will lose their freedom
and independence once in a relationship with you.
Over time he may resent you or drag his feet regarding
commitment.

~~~

MAKE IT HIS IDEA

Men tend to flee the relationship
when they feel a sense
of duty or commitment that wasn't his idea.
A man loves to do things for you all the time; he just
wants it to be his idea.

Try this:
"I could really use your help with something,
what do you think?"

Your man will be excited to *volunteer* for the job
and he'll feel as though he saved the day.

But when we come at him with our *to do* lists,
he feels …obligated.
As humans we tend to not enjoy things so much
when we're obligated.

Give him the invitation, then you'll get your
to do list done
and he won't feel nagged or pressured.

~~~

WEAR YOUR PINK HAT

A man wants a woman!

He doesn't want a female posing as a man,
involved in every aspect of his life.
He wants you to have your own activities and interests
and enjoys hearing about how they make you feel.

~~~

TAKE A NO WALLS APPROACH

When we are afraid of sharing our negative feelings
with him, he senses it
and tends to emotionally pull away.

All through your date he'll know something is wrong
and feel emotionally unsafe.
He may even think you're being fake or superficial, and
put up a wall toward you for the evening.

We must share our negative feelings with him, even if
they are upsetting.
He truly wants to know.

He longs to keep the emotional safety in the
relationship
and will grow closer even through the negative
emotions.

~~~

Communication helps a man feel respected.
When he doesn't feel respected he may emotionally
disconnect from the dating relationship.

~~~

CHECK HIS MOTIVES WHILE DATING

After a few dates if a man isn't asking deep questions in attempt to get to know you
or he's only taking you to noisy places or movies where you can't have a deep conversation,
you're either in the *friends only* category or the *I hope I get lucky* category.

If you're not into a *for now* relationship
with this man, run!

He's clearly not interested in a deep committed
relationship with you.

A man who is interested in you will deeply desire to get
to know the inner you.

~~~

IS HE TUNING OUT OF THE RELATIONSHIP?

How to spot if he's going cold on the relationship.

He is listening less.
He desires more time on his own.
He responds less to your needs.
He has stopped initiating romance, affection, sex, or
touching you.
He doesn't seem excited to be with you.

~~~

A man has pulled away from the relationship if you find yourself doing the following:

Serving him more.
Being clingy.
Dressing extra sexy to lure him back.
Initiating the commitment talk with him
(that includes hinting).
Going into *fix-it* mode with regard to the relationship.
Obsessing about him when you're not with him.
Checking his phone or email to see what he's been up to (suspicion).

~~~

ARGUMENTS

Never take the bait of getting into an
all out argument with a man.

Tell him the situation feels overwhelming, confusing
or whatever feeling you're experiencing
at that moment.
Let him know (without raising your voice)
that you would like to hear his feelings on the matter
later when it's calm.
Then, walk away to another room or somewhere else.

The mature man will come to you
and initiate talking after a brief time apart
because men have a deep need to feel things
are ok again.

The immature man will follow you, get angrier,
or blame you for needing time to sort your feelings.

An immature man is not ready for a relationship. Run!

WRAPPING IT UP

I hope my tips have helped you discover that it's not about finding a man to fill the void in your life, rather it's about defining who you are, finding your personal path in life, and living as though each day matters. I understand what it's like to get caught up in finding a man so I wouldn't feel alone. When I first learned the basics of dating I felt overwhelmed with thoughts that I may never find a quality man. The positive side of all this is that I began a healthy relationship with myself. I learned to love myself for who I am and the qualities that I possess. I gave myself a tune up and in the process the deep craving that I *must* have a man in my life, dissipated. Now I feel comfortable with myself and I live my life fully by enjoying time with my friends and activities that bring me joy. I'm not going to lie to you and say I never get lonely and that some nights seem excruciatingly long, but I'm happy inside and no amount of loneliness can take that away.

It wasn't until I fully understood the importance of having my own life and finding my personal identity that I realized I didn't need a man to feel valued, loved, and important. The key to healthy dating is clearly defining who you are as a woman and discovering your purpose in this world, then living each day with intention. Men love a woman who has her own interests and life and will naturally be drawn toward you. The unbearable loneliness you once feared will vanish as you create a life for yourself, filled with individuals who truly appreciate your uniqueness. Wouldn't you rather be happy and occasionally lonely than married and completely lonely! The point is once we discover who we are as women, we no longer feel desperate to capture a man.

The power of dating truly belongs to you. Never let a man determine the outcome of your choices, values, or life as I did. First decide who you are and if you even want a man in your life. If you do, you now have the ability to choose the perfect man for you. A single moment in time has the potential to change the outcome of the rest of your life. Choose your moments wisely and share your time with those who add value to who you are created to be.

Don't let one single moment in life define who you are. The purpose with which you live your life determines your outcome of your life!

The way you live your life and the people you include in your journey, add to the definition of who you are! You are the only one who can transform yourself into the unique woman you desire to be. Nothing will ever come close to the relationship you develop with yourself. Let today be the day you decide that you're worth waiting for a man who will treat you with love, compassion, respect, honor, and trust.

I wish you the very best on your journey and welcome your questions and letters. For more information, to inquire about life coaching packages, or to register for classes and seminars, please check out my website *Theultimatedatingschool.com.* We're in this together as women and I can't wait to hear your success stories. Finish strong and finish well!

CPSIA information can be obtained at www.ICGtesting.com
Printed in the USA
BVOW09s0044190914

367458BV00006B/11/P